Pressure Canning Recipes Cookbook

The Complete Beginners Guide for Learning How to Pressure Can and Preserve Vegetables, Meat, Soups, and More in a Jar with Tested Homemade Recipes

By

Fiona Begum

Disclaimer

This publication is designed to provide competent and reliable information regarding the subject matter covered. However, the views expressed in this publication are those of the author alone, and should not be taken as expert instruction or professional advice. The reader is responsible for his or her own actions.

The author hereby disclaims any responsibility or liability whatsoever that is incurred from the use or application of the contents of this publication by the purchaser or reader. The purchaser or reader is hereby responsible for his or her own actions.

Table of Contents

Introduction

Pressure canning can be overwhelming, particularly if you are new to it. However, it is worth considering. Learning the use of a pressure canner to safely can food with low acidic levels, such as meat, soups, and vegetables, is important. Don't restrict yourself to water bath canning pickles, jams, and jellies!

Pressure canning can be overwhelming at first. Though I was conversant with water bath canning for several years, I was still anxious when I operated a pressure canner for the first time. Several questions such as did I do it properly? Is this pressure canner safe? Will I set the kitchen ablaze? Kept on popping up in my mind.

After several years of pressure canning, I am delighted to have taken that bold step. To begin pressure canning your food at home, you need to know how the pressure canner works.

Recently, cases of botulism resulting in deaths continue to increase across the United States. Even though these deaths are avoidable, they occurred mostly because the wrong method of food preservation was adopted.

Clostridium botulinum in preserved foods can be fatal and lead to death when consumed. However, this is preventable when you follow the guidelines of pressure canning.

This book, *Pressure Canning Recipes Cookbook*, provides a complete guide on the nitty-gritty of pressure canning, such as how to get started with pressure canning, avoiding common pressure canning mistakes, pressure canning faqs, and recipes for vegetables, soups, stocks, and broths among others.

Adhering to the recipe steps described in this book will not only help prevent health complications from botulism or an imminent kitchen accident resulting from an explosion but give you insights and easy explanations of the practices you can engage in to adequately and safely pressure can your foods.

Without further ado, let's get started.

Chapter 1

Pressure Canning Basics

What Is Pressure Canning?

Pressure canning is used to preserve foods with low acidic contents, such as vegetables, meat, poultry, and seafood. This method of food preservation is considered the safest when preserving foods with low acidic contents.

How Does It Work?

A pressure canner utilizes pressure to produce temperatures higher than the boiling point to effectively heat-process foods with low acidic contents like beans, meat, soups, and vegetables. For the canning of pickles,

Jams, and other foods with high acidic levels (PH less than 4.6), boiling water canning is recommended.

From high school, we know the boiling point of water to be 100° C (212° F), at a minimum of sea level. At greater elevations, boiling of water is attained at lower temperatures, diminishing by 1° F for every 500 ft in elevation gained due to reduction in pressure at greater altitudes. The reverse is the case for a pressure canner, and a higher boiling temperature is attained by increased pressure.

Most foods are processed at a pressure of 10 pounds, which is approximately 240° F at sea level. Pressure has to be increased to achieve an exact result for higher altitudes.

When processed foods with low acidic levels are sealed properly in a pressure canner, they become stable on the shelf and can be stored for longer periods.

Quick Facts

- *According to research, the US Department of Agriculture declared pressure canning the safest means of preserving foods with low-acid levels in 1917.*

- *According to <u>research</u>, the first-ever tin canister for the preservation of food worldwide was created by Peter Durand in 1810.*
- *According to a <u>survey</u>, one in every five households in the United States practiced home canning of foods.*
- *According to <u>statistics</u>, family and friends (51.2%) are the most popular sources of pressure canning instructions, followed by cookbooks (16.7%).*
- *<u>Research</u> suggests that the most commonly canned foods are vegetables and tomatoes, with 64.9% and 59.2%, respectively.*
- *According to <u>research</u>, the number of people canning tomatoes continues to decrease, while the number of people canning vegetables is increasing.*

Reasons To Pressure Can Your Food

Canners Can Save You Money

Pressure canning your food can save you money in several ways. Vegetables from your garden that can't be stored in the freezer can be pressure canned. If hunting is your forte or your spouse's, you can pressure can the leftovers you cannot store in the freezer. If you have discounts on fruits, meat, and vegetables and come across deals, you can buy them in bulk and pressure can them.

Pressure Canners Save Your Time

Your meals can be prepared in bulk instead of one at a time, and the leftovers can be pressure canned, saving you time and stress of preparing meals now and then. However, when preparing your meals, ensure to use ingredients that can be canned safely.

When you pressure can your food, it reduces the time you spend on cooking and defrosting frozen meals.

Pressure Canners Save Energy

Besides saving you time and money, pressure canners save you energy. When your meals are prepared in bulk, you can pressure can it and simply warm the jars when needed. This reduces the energy exerted in cooking or defrosting frozen foods.

Pressure Canning Is Environmental Friendly

Another reason you should pressure can is that it is environmentally friendly. When you purchase processed food from stores, more package wastes are created, but using the packages as preservation jars helps to reduce environmental waste.

Pressure Canners Can Preserve More Of Your Harvest

Harvests from your garden like vegetables, beans, and fruits can be pressure canned which allows you to preserve space in your freezer and prevents your harvest from wastage. Preserving your harvests can be done through water bath canning, freezing, dehydrating, or freezing. However, pressure canning offers you a whole new level of preservation.

Pressure Canning Allows You To Preserve A Lot Of Food At Once

Stacking your pint jars is easy and simple when you pressure can, giving you the opportunity to can about 16-18 jars per batch, but two canners will double the amount. The leftovers can easily be canned for salads, pasta dishes, casseroles, and meat if you get a bargain on meat.

Pressure Canning Allows You To Know Exactly What Is In Your Food

Many things are added to processed foods, such as preservatives, GMOs, and additives. How much of these things are added to these processed foods, do you know? When you make a canned beef stew with potatoes, onions, peas, and carrots in your home, you

13

know exactly what you are eating. However, with processed foods, you never can tell what is in them.

Is Pressure Canning Dangerous?

Many people have erroneously held that pressure canning is risky and deadly; different stories of people dying from botulism due to improper canning and kitchen explosions scare people off from practicing pressure canning at home. However, pressure canning is safe and simple to practice if you adhere to the safety guidelines.

From findings, botulism from home-canned food cases are caused by defiance of instructions, early pull out of food, and water bath canning foods instead of pressure canning them.

Food preservation and canning are complimentary with homesteading and being autonomous, it is safe and simple. It doesn't matter if you're water bath canning jams, fruits, pickles, and jellies or through dehydration, fermentation, or freezing; they are all easy and simple to follow through.

If you follow through with the steps and instructions stated in a tested pressure canning recipe, the probability of things going bad during and after the preservation process is next to none.

Foods That Can Be Pressure Canned

Canned Food

Most foods can safely and easily be canned using a pressure canner but not with a water bath canner. Foods can be pressure canned because of their low acidic level. Using a pressure canner for their processing is safer. This can be done to reduce the products in your freezer.

Vegetables

Most vegetables are safe for pressure canning. However, ensure you follow the canning procedures for vegetables when preparing and processing the food. Examples of vegetables that can be pressure canned include; green beans, spinach, peas, carrots, potatoes, peppers, asparagus, corn, and beets.

Meat, Poultry, And Seafood

Meat, poultry, and seafood can be processed in a pressure canner. Ensure you follow the guidelines for adequate cooking. Caution should be taken when canning meat, and retail canners have the necessary equipment for heating compared to home canners, ensure the exterior of the fish or meat is heated properly before canning.

Stocks

Chicken and other poultry stocks are safe for processing using a pressure canner; ensure the fat is reduced to the minimum before canning.

Foods Not Safe To Can At All

Foods that prevent the destruction of microorganisms during the canning process are not appropriate for home canning. Foods that impede heat transfer during processing allow bacteria to live and are unsuitable for canning.

The procedures for canning some food products are available on the internet. However, caution should be taken in ensuring they are from reliable sources such as the National Center for Home Food Preservation, USDA guide to home canning, and Cooperative Extension websites in states across the US.

Dairy Products

Dairy products should not be pressure canned but frozen. Dairy products are low in acidic levels and aid the growth of Clostridium botulinum spores at room temperature.

The use of dairy products in canned recipes like meat gravy, custard pie filling mixes, pasta and cheese, and creamed soups should be frozen or prepared fresh instead.

Butter, Cheese, or Milk

The refrigeration of melted butter until solid does not involve heat and is unsafe for room temperature storage. The methods describing this process on the internet are not pressure canning, even though some directions call for heating or oven drying the butter. However, there is no research to validate canning in an oven has adequate heat to destroy harmful bacteria. There is also the risk of the jars breaking, which can lead to injury.

In a boiling water bath, melting cheese cubes in jars inside an oven at low temperature for certain minutes is unsafe. During the process of canning, water may be added, allowing spores to grow, making it unsafe. Dry hard cheese can curb the growth of bacteria which makes them waxed and stored on the shelf for long periods safely. The water level in soft cheeses is high, aiding the growth of botulism, causing bacteria, and being unsuitable for storage at room temperature.

Generally, the use of dairy products in canning recipes should be avoided and not added to soups intended for canning.

Eggs

The recipes for the home cooking of pickled or plain eggs for shelf storage have not been validated by research. The commercial production of pickled eggs requires meeting the USDA and the Department of Agriculture across different states for the acidic level of the product.

Oil

Placing oil coats in food or herbs can result in the growth of Clostridium botulinum. Do not seal fresh vegetables, fruits, or herbs; put oil in a jar or bottle for storage at room temperature.

Starch

During the process of canning, starch interferes with the transfer of heat. Avoid using it except scientifically certified. Thickening soups, clear gel, tapioca relishes, pie fillings with flour, cornstarch, or other starches should be avoided except if included in a scientifically tested recipe.

Pasta and Rice

Rice, pasta, or noodles should not be added to canned products because the starch interferes with the transfer of heat to the center of the jar; rather, can products like chicken broth or spaghetti sauce and the noodles or pasta should be added when you are ready to serve the food.

Very Dense Purees

The density of purees impedes heat from reaching the cold spot in the jar, making it unsuitable for canning.

Can pumpkins or squash cubes instead of winter squash, mashed or pureed pumpkin.

Can rehydrate dried beans instead of pureed cooked dried beans (refried beans).

Can small potatoes instead of mashed potatoes.

You can drain the canned food and puree or mash it when ready for use, and pureed products can be frozen safely.

Bread and Cakes in a Jar

Bread and cakes have low acidic levels and aid the growth of Clostridium botulinum which can lead to poisoning from botulism. If bread and cakes baked in glass jars are sealed with canning lids, they become unsafe upon removal from the oven.

Tender products

Do not pressure can tender products if the process will affect the product's quality.

Other Products

Broccoli

Cauliflower (except pickled)

Egg Plant

Summer Squash

Rules for Safe Pressure Canning

- Pressure can all foods with low acidic levels, such as meat, vegetables, etc. Do not water bath can low acidic foods
- Never use a pressure cooker for home pressure canning. Always use a pressure canner when canning low acidic foods.
- Be familiar with the brand and model of your pressure canner so you can safely operate it.
- Perform a test spin on your pressure canner before planned canning.
- Follow a tested recipe.
- Handle jars with care. Always use a jar lifter to place filled jars onto the rack.
- Use aluminum foil for cleaning when pressure canning and covering your work surfaces.
- Use an outdoor deep fryer not to heat up the kitchen.
- Adjust the heat and build the pressure.
- The accuracy of your timing should be spot on by ensuring you maintain an even pressure throughout the duration of your process time
- Adjust for altitude accordingly to increase or decrease the amount of pressure (not the cooking time) when canning your food. More on altitude adjustments are discussed in chapter 2.

- After pressure canning, allow the pressure on the pressure canner to cool off naturally without speeding up the process by running cold running water on the external part of the canner.
- Upon the depressurization of the canner, weights from vent pipes should be removed, petcock opened, lids loosened, and jars removed after considerable time has passed, roughly 12-24 hours.

Chapter 2

Canning Glossary of Terms

Acetic acid: This is the main acid in vinegar, which is a strong, transparent liquid (vinegar is 5 percent acetic acid). Vinegar is sour because of acetic acid.

Ascorbic acid: This is the scientific term for vitamin C, a soluble vitamin found in nature and is sold to the public as white, odorless powder or crystals. It serves as an antioxidant to prevent oxidation and keep fruits and vegetables that are light-colored from browning.

Bacteria: There are microscopic organisms that can be hazardous and are present in the soil, water, and air surrounding. Some bacteria produce poisons that must be eliminated by heating to 240°F (116°C) for a predetermined period of time because they flourish in preserved foods that are low in acids. Low-acid foods must therefore be canned in a pressure canner.

Botulism: Food poisoning brought on by consuming poisons caused by the bacteria Clostridium botulinum. Botulism may result in death. The spores of this bacteria are typically found in the soil, wind, and dust that clings to raw food. They are a member of a group of bacteria incapable of growing in the presence of air and typically do not flourish in foods high in acidity. Any firmly closed jar of low-acid food yet to undergo the proper processing can support the growth of the spores. Toxin-producing spores can be eliminated by processing low-acid foods at the proper temperature and length of time.

Browning: The unpleasant change in color brought on when some fruits and vegetables' cut surfaces are exposed to oxygen in the atmosphere. Oxidation is the name of the reaction.

Canner: One of two items of equipment used in fresh preservation to process jars with food products inside and enclosed with two-piece lids on top. Boiling water canners for high-acid foods and pressure canners for low-acid foods are the two canner types suggested for use while preserving fresh foods.

Citrus acid: An organic acid that comes from citrus fruits like lemons and limes. It is offered as white crystals or granules. It is a component of commercial produce protectors that prevents oxidation, as well as pectin products that help gel formation by raising the acidity of jam or jelly.

Dial-gauge pressure canner: A pressure canner with a gauge and pressure regulator to visibly show the right pressure level.

Weighted-gauge pressure canner: A style of pressure canner with pressure settings of 5, 10, and 15 lb (35, 69, and 103 kPa), and either a 3 or 1-piece weight unit. (For fresh preservation, only 10- and 15-lb/69 and 103 kPa pressure weights are utilized. Although not for preserving, the 5-lb/35 kPa weight is used for cooking.) The weight(s) rock when the level of pressure has been reached or is being sustained is caused because steam has been used up during the processing period

Fresh preservation: This is when fresh produce and freshly made foods are preserved in glass jars with lids and bands using heat to eliminate the microorganisms responsible for spoilage. This terminology is also used to describe home canning.

Headspace: The empty area in a jar between the liquid or food at the top and the lid's bottom. For food to expand while the jars are heated and for a solid vacuum seal to form when the jars cool, the proper amount of headspace is necessary.

Home canning: This involves employing heat processing to eliminate bacteria that causes rot so as to preserve freshly prepared foods in glass jars with two-piece closures.

Hot-pack technique: This involves putting hot, preheated food into jars before they are heat-processed in a canner. Food that has been preheated releases extra air, enables a tighter pack in the jar, and lessens floating. When it comes to hard foods, this method is recommended over the raw-pack technique.

Raw-pack technique: Putting raw, unheated food into jars before heating it

kPa (kilopascal): A measure of atmospheric pressure in metric units

Mason jar: A glass jar that is very appropriate for boiling water or pressure canning heat-processed foods and/or liquids. Mason jars are made to resist the high temperatures and repeated use involved in fresh preservation. True mason jars also adhere to a set of dimensions and weights in line with approved safe heat processing procedures. The jars come in sizes ranging from 4 ounces (125 mL) to 1 quart.

Heat processing or processing: To altogether remove enzymes and eliminate dangerous molds, yeasts, and bacteria, food must be heated to a specific temperature and for a specific amount of time in filled jars. All foods that are home-preserved require heat processing to maintain food safety. Bacteria that are inherently present in food and/or enter the jar during filling are destroyed during processing. It also enables gases or air to be expelled from the jar to produce an airtight vacuum seal as the food cools, eliminating food recontamination.

Process time: The period of time full jars are heated in a pressure canner or boiling water canner. The processing time has to be adequate to heat the coolest area in the jar. Every contemporary, tested fresh recipe includes a processing time that is dependent on various variables like acidity, food product type, and jar size.

Venting:

1. Using heat to force air to exit from a sealed jar. When a substance is heated, such as food or liquid, it extends upward and expels air from the jar via the build-up of pressure in the headspace.
2. Allowing air to exit from a pressure canner.

Chapter 3

Getting Started With Pressure Canning

Types of Pressure Canners

Dial Gauge Pressure Canner

Dial gauge pressure canners are the most popular canners in the market because they are affordable, diverse in sizes, and their replaceable components are not difficult to find. These canners usually operate at 11 pounds pressure (altitude dependent). During heating and processing, the pressure level is indicated by the dial at the center of the lid. Manual heat source adjustment is required for the canner to process at 11 pounds (not more or less).

Testing of the dial gauge has to be carried out yearly. The gauge must be consistently checked when processing to ensure the right pressure level's stability.

Weighted Gauge Pressure Canner

Weighted gauge pressure canners convert dial gauge canners by adding a weighing set (usually 5lb, 10lb, and 15lb). Rather than use a dial gauge for pressure level reading, the pressure is read by listening for the rocky movement of the weight to determine the attainment of the pressure level (for example, 15lbs based on your altitude). One great advantage of weighted pressure canners is their self-pressure regulation capability; checking the dial gauge is not necessary.

Parts of a Pressure Canner

Weighted gauge and dial gauge pressure canners come with a base pot and a jar rack, and the pot for either pressure canner is the same. The pot is deep, and the lid is attached to it.

The Lid

The lid is an important part of pressure canners, both weighted gauge and dial gauge pressure canners have lids. In a weighted gauge, the weight is placed at the lid's center, and other pressure canner components, such as the overpressure plug and the vent lock, are fixed on the lid's edges. In a dial gauge, the dial is placed at the center of the lid and on the edge of the lid is the vent pipe.

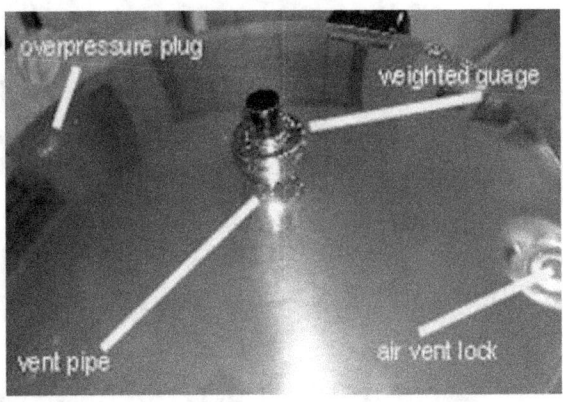

Air Vent Lock

The air vent lock creates an opening for the passage of air or exhaust at the start of the processing duration. The air vent lock moves up to seal the passage as pressure increases. The vent lock also functions as a safety device for preventing accidental lid opening when there are remnants of pressure in the canner. However, you cannot remove the lid until the pressure finally drops, making the lid a fail-safe.

Steams stream off the vent pipe, even after the vent lock is closed. It is important to allow the steams to escape entirely in compliance with the recommendation of the venting time, not more than 10 minutes most times.

Vent Pipe

In a dial gauge, the vent pipe accommodates the counterweight (weight is placed on the vent pipe); this is different from the position the dial sits in and relies on the dial to determine the pressure.

In the weighted gauge, the weight is placed in the vent pipe and relies on the weights to determine the pressure. The weights, as mentioned above, differ for each type of pressure canner. Before every use, adequately check the vent openings to confirm they are clear. You can do the checks by looking through or inserting a string through the openings to remove any blockage.

Weights

Each type of pressure has a different weight. When the selected pressure is attained, the weight makes a rocking motion indicating the attainment of the expected pressure level.

Single weight for a dial gauge   All American weighted gauge   Presto weighted gauge

Dial Gauge Pressure Canner Weight

The weight in a dial gauge pressure canner is used for closing off the vent to enable the build-up of pressure. However, the volume of pressure is not determined by the weight. The dial is observed to ascertain when the desired pressure level is attained; then, the heat level is adjusted to maintain the level on the dial.

Weighted Gauge Pressure Canner Weight

In a weighted gauge, the pressure level is restricted to 5lb, 10lb, or 15lb. The dial is not relied upon; rather, the weight is selected based on the altitude. The recipe determines the level of pressure needed.

Overpressure Plug

The overpressure plug is a small plug made of rubber. It is majorly a safe means of releasing pressure. If the pressure level becomes too high, the overpressure plug opens up and allows the passage of steam. It comes with a loud noise, and you might be startled. However, the canner does not explode.

Both dial gauge and the weighted gauge pressure canners have an overpressure plug.

Sealing Ring or Gasket

Not all pressure canners have a sealing ring or rubber gasket. Canners like Presto and Mirro come with a sealing ring inside the rim. The sealing ring tightens the seal, thereby allowing the build-up of pressure.

Canners without rubber gaskets are equipped with lids close down tightly, not requiring a seal. However, you should lubricate the lid often. The maintenance and care for the canners are always included in the pack.

Tools and Supplies for Pressure Canning

For pressure canning, you need tools and supplies like;

- Pressure canner (not a pressure cooker). Per the size and quality, a pressure canner could go for 100 - 500 dollars.
- Canning bands, jars, and lids. Lids for single use cost around $3-$4 for twelve, and quart-sized jars cost about a dollar per one. Canning jars and bands are reusable, but lids are not.

  Note: Several recipes call for the use of quart or pint jars. Ensure that the size jar indicated in the individual recipe is used instead. Popular brands are mason or ball jars.

- Other useful canning accessories include; jar lifter, potholders, ladle, canning funnel (wide-mouth), kitchen towels, magnetic lid-lifter, digital timer, and a canning rack if your pressure canner did not come with a rack. The canning rack is placed at the bottom of pressure canners, enabling the jars not to touch the bottom of the pressure canner.

- You will also need gas or a traditional stove with coil heating units. Using a stove with a smooth top is not recommended and may be unsafe. Confirm with the manufacturer if your stove model can pressure can.

Step-By-Step Pressure Canning Process
Step 1

Ensure the pressure canner is in a good working condition before you begin the preparation of your food. Follow the manufacturer's procedure for cleaning the lid gaskets and other parts of your pressure canner; ensure the vent pipes are obstruction free and no materials or mineral deposits are trapped. Place the canner over the center of the burner but ensure the burner and range are in the same level. If the heat from the burner is too much, the pressure canner will be damaged. Generally, you should not use a gas range burner or an outdoor LP gas burner above 12,000 BTUs. Go through the manufacturer's directions for the instructions on the right burners for your pressure canner.

Place the rack and hot water in the pressure canner. If the quantity of water used is not stated for a particular food, use sufficient water a few inches higher in the canner. For long processing, more water is needed. Some food products like smoked fish require the beginning of the processing with more volume of water in the pressure canner.

You can adjust the water to 180° F if the food is packed hot before processing. However, take care to prevent the decrease of the water depth due to over boiling or overheating. You can adjust to 140° F if the food is packed raw.

Step 2

Put the filled jars alongside the lids and ring bands fitted on the jar rack inside the pressure canner using a jar lifter. When using a jar lifter to move the jars, ensure the jar lifter is placed in a secure position beneath the neck of the jar (below the ring band of the lid). Ensure the jar is in an upright position always. If the jar is tilted, it will spill the food into the sealing section of the lid.

Step 3

Tighten the pressure canner lid firmly, open the petcock or place the weight on the vent pipe.

Step 4

Adjust the heat setting to the highest ranking, and heat the water until it boils. Steams will flow freely through the vent pipe or petcock in the shape of a funnel.

Without adjusting the heat setting, allow the steam to flow for 10 minutes.

Step 5

When the venting of the pressure canner is over, the weighted gauge or counterweight should be placed on the vent pipe or simply close the petcock. The pressurizing of the canner will be done within 3-10 minutes.

Step 6

When the dial gauge shows that the desired pressure level has been attained, begin the timing of the process. If the canner does not have a dial gauge, begin the timing of the process when the weighted gauge moves in a rocking motion or as described by the manufacturer.

Step 7

Regulate the heat under the pressure canner to keep a consistent level at or a little above the right pressure gauge. Some weighted gauges jiggle several times every minute, while others may rock slowly through the entire process. For the right indication, check the directions stated by the manufacturer.

Important Things To Note

- Underprocessing or foods that are unsafe can be a result of pressure loss at any time.
- Moisture may be lost from the jars if there is an immediate and large pressure difference during the processing.
- If the pressure level falls below the required volume, initiate pressure back to the canner and start the timing afresh (use the original processing time). This has to be done to ensure the safety of the food.

Step 8

After completing the timing process, the heat should be turned off, unmount the pressure canner from the heat if possible, and allow it to cool. (To move the pressure canner, lift it and do not slide. You can leave the pressure canner at a spot after turning off the heat. This is done to prevent the jars inside the pressure canner from tilting over if it is not easy to move about.)

When the timed process is completed, turn off the heat, remove the canner from the heat (electric burner) if possible, and let the canner cool down naturally. (Lift the canner to move it; do not slide the canner. It is also okay to leave the canner in place after you have turned off the burner. It is better to do so than to let jars inside the canner tilt or tip over if the canner is too heavy to move easily.)

As the pressure canner cools, it also depressurizes. Allow this cooling to occur naturally, not forcefully. The food may be spoiled if forcefully cooled. Examples of forced cooling include opening the vent pipe before depressurization. Besides food spoilage, forced cooling will lead to moisture loss from jars and seal failure. The pressure canner lid may also be warped if forced cooling is done.

Take caution while removing the weight on the vent pipe after cooking, even if the dial gauge canner reads 0lbs. Before removing it, you should carefully tilt the weight slightly to ensure the steam doesn't escape. New brands of canner come with a lid or handle cover lock, ensure the canner cools off before twisting the lids off. The lid should not be forced open until the cover locks are released. The manufacturers provide more information based on the model.

Timing should depressurize older pressure canner models with no dial gauge. To depressurize standard size canners that are heavy-walled, wait for at least 30 minutes when they are loaded with pints and when loaded with quarts, wait for 45 minutes. New pressure canners' thin-walled models cool off faster and are designed with vent locks for opening when the pressure is gone. The depressurization of these canners is complete when the piston in the vent lock returns to its original position. However, some of the locks are built-in handles making them invisible. When the locks are released, the lid opens.

Step 9

When the depressurization of the canner is completed, remove the weight from the vent pipe, and open the petcock. After waiting for 10 minutes, carefully unfasten the lid and remove it. Lift the lid and the underside away from where you are to prevent a burn on your face due to the steam escaping from the canner.

Step 10

Use a jar lifter to remove the jars one after the other, be careful to prevent the tilting of the jars. Place the jars in a cooling rack or a towel carefully, ensure a minimum space of an inch is left between the jars when cooling, and do not place the jars on a cold surface.

Step 11

While the jars cool off, allow them to sit without disturbance between 12-24 hours. Avoid tightening the ring bands on the lids or pushing down the center of the flat metal lid until the jar cools off.

Step 12

Remove the ring bands from the sealed jars. Refrigerate any jar that is not sealed and use them first. You can wash, dry, and reuse ring bands when pressure canning next time.

Step 13

All leftovers on the jars and lids should be removed by washing.

Step 14

The jars should be labeled and stored in a cool, dry place where light cannot reach.

Step 15

Dry the canner, lid, and gasket. The petcocks and safety valves should be removed, washed, and dried adequately. You should follow the manufacturer's instructions for the maintenance and storage of your pressure canner.

Adjusting Altitude For Home Canning

Before starting the pressure canning process, it is vital to know the altitude of where you live. For instance, South Dakota's altitude range is between 1,200-6,000 ft. above sea level. A person living in an area of 1,200 ft. would have to increase the processing time by 5 minutes in a boiling water bath canner, for instance. The increased processing time ensures the killing of pathogenic agents, thereby keeping the canned food safe. Instead of increasing the processing time when pressure canning, the pounds of pressure are increased. The table below gives the required time adjustments following the altitude.

The processing time should not be decreased in any pressure canners. To find the altitude of your locality, go to your local planning commission, zonal office, or a website about your city. Alternatively, you can download the Altimeter App to find the altitude of your locality or by checking the website, www.whatismyelevation.com.

BOILING WATER BATH CANNERS

Feet Above Sea Level	Increase in Processing Time
1,001-3,000	5 minutes
3,001-6,000	10 minutes
6,001-8,000	15 minutes
8,001-10,000	20 minutes

PRESSURE CANNERS

Feet Above Sea Level	Weighted-Gauge (Pounds of Pressure)	Dial-Gauge (Pounds of Pressure)
0-1,000	10	11
1,001-2,000	15	11
2,001-3,000	15	12
3,001-6,000	15	13
6,001-8,000	15	14
8,001-10,000	15	15

44

Chapter 4

Avoiding Common Pressure Canning Mistakes

A few of the most common problems that may arise from your pressure canner are discussed below.

Not Adjusting the Pressure or Canning Time for Your Altitude

The pressure for pressure canning or the canning time for boiling water bath canning needs to be adjusted if you live above 1,000 ft above sea level. Keep in mind that at higher altitudes, water does not boil at the same temperature as that of the sea level. These adjustments address that, which ensures your food is safely preserved.

Overfilling the Jars

An inch down to a half-inch of head space should be left, according to good canning recipes. That is the distance between the food's upper surface and the jar's rim. The canning lids won't seal if the jars are filled too high. However, the food can be eaten right away, moved to the refrigerator and used in a week, or processed again with just enough headspace and fresh lids. Nevertheless, you'll lose a lot of time. Better to start with the proper amount of headspace.

Reusing Canning Lids

Canning lids are not intended for repeated usage. Even though they can be reused and resealed, there is no assurance the seal will remain intact because the sticky rubber on the bottom of the lid wears down quickly. Again, having several unsealed jars would not be worth the cost, especially considering that canning lids hardly cost more than $3 each box. Save the old lids in a different bag; Usually, they are used for leftovers stored in the refrigerator.

Tattler is an exception to this rule when it comes to canning lids. These lids feature replaceable rubber seals and are designed to be reused.

Forgetting to Clean the Jar's Edges

Cleaning the jar's edges is, in my opinion, one of the key tasks in canning. Pieces from whatever you're making wind up on the edges when you fill the jars. The lids will not seal if you do not clean the edges and place the seals over the top of the food pieces.

Correcting this canning error is simple. Before putting the lid on top and tightening the rings, clean the jar's edges with a moist cloth or paper towel. You won't forget to do it if you incorporate it into your routine for canning.

Liquid Loss or Siphoning

Several factors can be responsible for fluid loss in the jars when pressure canning, the two most predominant reasons why fluid loss occurs are improper tightening of lids or a small headspace.

If there is insufficient headspace, a fluid loss can occur when the food inside the can bubbles upward, thereby hitting the lid and displacing it. Untightened lids lead to fluid loss in the same manner. If the lid is loose, the boiling liquid mix with the venting air from the jars and escape, thereby leading to fluid loss.

Conversely, a fluid loss will not lead to food safety problems. According to the National Center For Food Preservation, fluid loss is not a problem provided it is not in "excess," that is, not above half of the entire liquid in the jar, which in such case is a minor problem. The food not covered by water may likely dry out or turn brown. However, food safety will not be a problem if the jar is sealed and the processing is properly executed.

Low water levels are common when pressure canning beans because beans can absorb the liquid, and there is a chance of liquid loss to siphoning. This makes the canning of dry beans while maintaining the water line difficult. The canned food is still safe, provided it is done the right way.

Broken Jars

Broken jars may be caused by little fragments or little deficiencies in the jar. This usually arises from thermal shock. Thermal shock is often caused by an abrupt change in the jar's temperature. The contents of the jar have to be warm or cool before the temperature can be adjusted if necessary.

The temperature of the pressure canner must match that of the food at the point of being placed inside the canner. Even if the food is boiling when poured into the jars, little temperature loss occurs before the food is placed inside the canner. If the food is raw, the temperature is not far from room temperature.

Note

For recipes that are raw pack, the water temperature in the pressure canner should be very hot (the temperature should be about 140 F).

For recipes that are hot pack, the water temperature in the pressure canner is around the boiling point (which is a temperature of about 180 F).

Unable to Remove the Lid After the Pressure Canner Has Cooled Off Completely

This pressure canner problem is most common when the gasket is old and needs lubrication. However, this is an indication that the gasket has to be replaced. Pending the replacement of the gasket, if you are sure your pressure canner cooled off completely but the lid remains unopen, gently hit the lid using a hammer and attempt to open the lid once more. To get the lid to open, you may try this several times or wait a few minutes before making another trial. To avoid future occurrences, you can lubricate the gasket with a small quantity of olive oil.

Floating Air Bubbles at the Top of The Jar After Removing the Jars from the Pressure Canner

Sometimes you may notice air bubbles drifting to the top of the jar when you have removed your jars from the pressure canner. You might wonder if you sealed the jars properly or feel concerned about the safety of your food. However, you need not worry as this is not unusual or harmful.

Sometimes you may notice air being released after your jars have been processed. There may be bubbles even up to one or two hours. This is not a major problem, except if the occurrence has been frequent for some days, fermentation or spoilage is possible in your jars. The best action in this situation will be to toss out the jars.

Untested Dial Gauge

If you are pressure canning, always use a tested dial gauge, which should be done annually. Sometimes your gauge may be giving you a reading that is not accurate. This is dangerous as processed food may be improperly canned and unsafe for consumption. You can use a weighted gauge or a jiggler to avoid this safety issue. Using any of these does not require testing, and you are assured of your pressure readings.

Ensure your pressure canning is always done at the appropriate pressure using a tested gauge or a weighted gauge (jiggler).

Quick Cooling Your Pressure Canner

When the processing time has elapsed, the canner takes some time to return to room pressure. Do not take the jars out of the pressure canner until it cools off completely.

The cooling process is a vital part of the canning process. Avoid hastening the process by submerging your canner in cold water, hitting the jiggler, or removing the weight entirely.

Submerging your pressure canner in cold water will alter the pressure abruptly, damaging the seals, jars cracking, or breaking down your pressure canner.

Storing Jars with the Rings Unremoved

The final canning error you should avoid is keeping the rings on the jars when storing the canned food. Making a mistake here is simple - you label and put the jars away after allowing them to sit on the shelves for 24 hours, and perhaps you forget to consider the rings.

What's wrong with storing jars with their rings on?

The lids can become loose and come undone even with the rings attached, enabling air and bacteria to penetrate beneath the lid. That may result in spoilage, which is concealed by the rings that are still attached to the jars. The pressure from the rings may occasionally force the lids to reseal.

You may quickly identify a jar with a poor seal by storing jars without their rings on. You'll be able to remove it from storage and throw it away immediately. Never consume food from a jar with a damaged seal since you can't be sure when it happened or what microorganisms might be there.

In addition, rust and mold are frequently seen under jar rings. Tiny amounts of liquid that escape the jar in the canning process may get caught under the ring, where it might remain moist and sweet. You might attempt to twist the ring some months later only to discover that it is stuck closed. (Or twist it off to reveal mold-covered threads).

A Short message from the Author:

Hey, I hope you are enjoying the book? I would love to hear your thoughts!

Many readers do not know how hard reviews are to come by and how much they help an author.

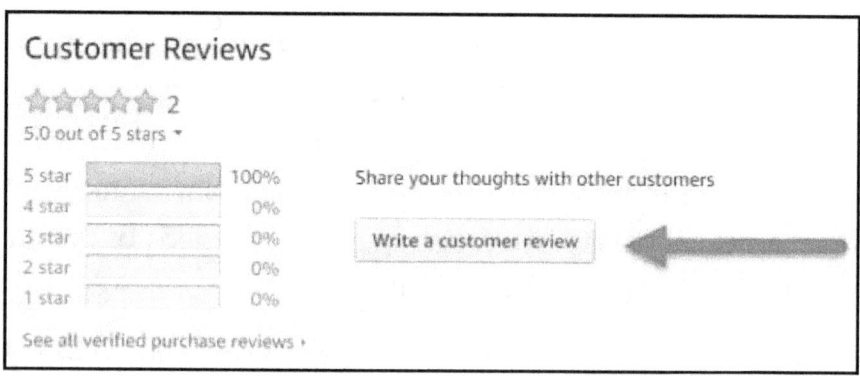

I would be incredibly grateful if you could take just 60 seconds to write a short review on Amazon, even if it is a few sentences!

>> Click here to leave a quick review

Thanks for the time taken to share your thoughts!

Chapter 5

Pressure Canning FAQs

Is There Any Way to Can Low-acid Foods Without Using Pressure?

Based on findings from the United States Department of Agriculture's (USDA) complete guide to home canning, the average time to safely process low-acid foods using a boiling water canner is between 7-11 hours. On the other hand, the average time it takes to pressure can low-acid foods is between 15-100 minutes.

If you have decided to boil something for as long as 11 hours, do note that the temperature will have to be kept constant for the entirety of the duration. If for some reason, such as an electricity blackout, flash off from gas, or wind blowing off the flame, the heat source is interrupted, the boiling water canner will not maintain the temperature, and the whole process will have to be started all over.

This will result in a waste of fuel, time, water, and stress that are avoidable in the first place if you had used a pressure canner and the canning had been done faster (in minutes, not hours).

It is noteworthy that the USDA has no publication outlining a canning process without pressure for foods that are low in acid. However, if you insist on processing your food without pressure, you are solely responsible for the aftermath.

Can I Use My Electric Pressure Cooker or Instant Pot to Pressure Can?

Sadly, some manufacturers of electric pressure cookers deceptively advertise their products as being able to safely pressure can foods. A particular company even said their electric multi-cooker complies with the USDA pressure canning standards. This led to NCHFP (an affiliate of USDA) posting a warning on their website instructing buyers against using this electric multi-cooker for canning.

According to the NCHFP's post, "Even if there are references to the National Center for Home Food Preservation in the directions for canning contained in the manufacturer's manual, we do not presently endorse using USDA's canning procedures in appliances such as the electric multi-cooker."

In the infomercial of the manufacturer of the electric multi-cooker, an actress is shown placing jars into the multi-cooker with the caption "Meets USDA standards for canning." However, the National Center for Home Food Preservation clearly states that it doesn't.

The manufacturer claimed their product attained the required temperature for pressure canning at 2,000 ft. and was compatible with four-quart jars. You may want to ask, What then is the problem? The product meets the USDA standards, doesn't it?

Electric pressure and multi-cookers are not safe for pressure canning for the following reasons;

On and Heat Cycles

Electric pressure cookers make use of a ceramic component for heating. This ceramic component automatically turns off when the required temperature or pressure is attained and back on when the temperature drops beneath a specified point. Pressure cookers in the same range can vary with a difference of one psi during the process. These pressure thresholds differ and can be predetermined by the manufacturer. The value of the least temperature attainable during the "off" cycle is unknown.

56

No Change in Altitude

The time required to process foods that are more than 2,000 ft. needs the pressure level to be increased. Still, the electric pressure and mufti-cookers presently available on the market cannot maintain pressure levels above 11 psi for a prolonged duration.

No Venting

In the assessment of all the instructions for pressure canning for all the electric pressure and multi-cookers, it was discovered that the instructions do not contain particular instructions for a thorough venting of the canner in compliance with the USDA-approved time of ten minutes before processing.

Not Stovetop

The USDA processing standards were formulated using a stovetop pressure canner, and data is unavailable to validate or invalidate the safety of pressure canning using electric pressure or multi-cookers. However, sufficient data regarding the dangers posed by botulism in foods that are not properly canned is available.

Even if the manufacturer of the electric pressure cooker insists and even validates the attainment of 15psi by their electric pressure cooker; for instance, the Instant Pot Max's mode of operation of electric pressure cookers (on and off cycles) does not provide a means for the verification of the maintenance of the temperature for the entirety of the processing duration.

Can I Process Jars of Different Size In the Pressure Canner?

If all the jars include an exact recipe but differ in size, the processing duration for the largest jars in the canner should be observed. Even if you have a one-quart jar and others are pints, the processing duration for the bigger quart jar should be observed if you cannot possibly pressure can another batch.

Nonetheless, it is always better to process the foods in different batches so that the foods contained in the smaller jars (pint jars) will not be over-processed.

Can I Process Jars with Different Contents (Some with Veggie and Some with Meat) In the Pressure Canner?

The best thing to do in this instance is to process each food content differently in batches. However, if your time is limited, processing jars with more than one content in the pressure canner is possible. Observe the processing duration for the jars containing the food content requiring the highest processing time. For instance, if you want to pressure can four jars of veggie stock (10 minutes) and a jar of beef stock (15 minutes), you will have to pressure can the entire food contents in the canner for the highest duration (15 minutes).

Note that the food contents requiring lesser processing duration might end up over-processing.

Do I Have to Test the Gauge of My Weighted Gauge Pressure Canner?

No, the weighted gauge pressure canner's weight is calibrated and accurate. Unless it is broken or damaged, the readings are correct.

What If My Pressure Canner that I Have Used for Years Goes Off?

If your pressure canner is not at the required level when processing, the food content in the jars will be of poor quality and be over-cooked, or the product will be unsafe before it is stored on the shelf. Clostridium botulinum is a microorganism that contaminates canned products; the germ that causes botulism survives only in an environment that is sealed. Airless at room temperature, a perfect medium to breed will be a canning jar. And the areas occupied by the danger-posing Clostridium botulinum expand unseen, without smell or taste.

How Do I Prevent My Pressure Canner from Explosion?

Reports of pressure canner explosion in different family histories are common, and some people will have different experiences to share. However, the modern pressure canner has several built-in safety precautions that prevent them from exploding.

It is important to check for these two things;

1. Ensure your pressure canner comes with safety valves that come off before excess pressure is built-up.

2. Ensure your vent pipe is cleared of obstruction from food particles and thoroughly cleaned. To do this, simply remove the weight and place the lid in a lighted area to check if light can pass through. If there is an obstruction, that indicates that something is obstructing the vent and must be cleared out before you continue.

Chapter 6

Recipes For Vegetables

Asparagus

Ingredients

- 10 pounds of asparagus
- Boiling water for packing
- Pickling and canning salt (this is optional)

Instructions

1. Get your pressure canner ready by bringing it up to temperature. While getting ready, prepare boiling water that will fill up the jars.

2. Trim the asparagus to a size appropriate for the jars (the size of a quart or lesser, broad mouth recommended).
3. To prepare a raw pack, trim the asparagus into appropriate size and pack them into the canning jars raw. To prepare a hot pack, the asparagus should be blanched in boiling water for three minutes and then packed.
4. You can add salt if you desire. The suggested quantities are one teaspoon per quart or ½ teaspoon per pint. However, if you don't take much salt, you can reduce it as salt is only optional.
5. Pour the boiling water on the asparagus inside the jars, leaving a one-inch headspace.
6. Then, begin processing your pressure canner at a pressure of 10 pounds for 30 or 40 minutes (pints or quarts). If you use 12 oz canning jars, use 30 minutes, and if you use 24 oz canning jars, use 40 minutes.

Do not forget the pressure modification to an altitude higher than 1,000 ft. Refer to the section on **Adjusting Altitudes for Home Canning** in chapter 2.

7. Finally, do not remove the jars from the pressure canner until it completely cools off. (Use a jar lifter to unload the jars).

Note

For altitudes greater than 1,000 ft., ensure you adjust your pressure appropriately. If a weighted gauge pressure canner is used, you need to adjust your settings to 15 pounds. Ensure to refer to the section on **Adjusting Altitudes for Home Canning** in chapter 2.

Beets

Ingredients

- Beets
- Salt (this is optional)
- Water

Instructions

1. Based on the manufacturer's recommendations, prepare your pressure canner. (Most pressure canner models follow the following directions; You add water to the bottom of your pressure canner, insert the trivet, and then bring the pressure canner to a simmer on the stove).
2. Wash the beets after the removal of the tops and tails.
3. Proceed to boil the beets between 14-30 minutes, depending on the size, until fully cooked. You can test if your beets are fully cooked using a fork.
4. The beets should be strained and allowed to cool to the extent of being handled.
5. Rub off the skins of the beets and rinse thoroughly.
6. Slice the beets in diameter of two inches and place the beets inside the jars, leaving a headspace of one inch. If the beets are large sizes, slice them into ½ inch.
7. If you desire salt, add for flavor (optional). Boil clean water and pour it over the beets inside the canning jars, maintaining the one space inch.

8. If air bubbles exist, remove them, adjust the headspace, and use two-part canning lids to cap.
9. Remove air bubbles, adjust headspace, and cap with 2-part canning lids.
10. Put the jars inside the pressure canner on the trivet and keep the lids capped.
11. For 10 minutes, allow the pressure canner to vent steam before you seal using the right weight. (Ensure you always follow the directions recommended by your pressure canner manufacturer).
12. Allow the pressure canner to attain the required pressure level, then maintain the required pressure by adjusting the temperature (turn down the heat). Process the jars for 30 minutes.
13. When the pressure canning duration is attained, turn off the heat and allow the pressure canner to cool off completely before you open it.
14. Take out the jars from the pressure canner using a jar lifter, and check the seals thoroughly. If there are improperly sealed jars, refrigerate and use them immediately.
15. All rightly sealed and canned jars of beets have a pantry shelf-life between 12-18 months.

Note

- For adjustments of altitudes, the duration of pressure canning remains unchanged even if the altitude changes. However, the pressure has to be increased when the altitude is higher. The average canning pressure for beets is 10 pounds. If the feet are above 1000, increase the pressure to 15 pounds.
- If you are using a dial gauge pressure canner, refer to the section on **Adjusting Altitudes for Home Canning** in chapter 2.
- The quantity yield depends majorly on the size of the beets and how they are packed in the jars. However, 20-22 pounds of beets yield a canner load of 7 quarts, and 13-15 pounds of beets field a canner load of 9 pints.
- When pressure canning, salt is only optional and not required. You may add ½ teaspoon for each pint or a teaspoon for each quart for flavor.

Carrots

Ingredients

- 16-18 lbs of carrots
- Salt (this is optional)

Instructions

1. Peel and chop the carrots (peeling is suggested because it significantly boosts the quality of the carrots). You should chop the size of the carrots to your regular meal size or any convenient size.
2. Prepare your pressure canner and warm the base of the canner with water (2-3 inches) with the base trivet set.
3. Boil water and place it next to the pressure canner.
4. If you prefer a hot pack, in the boiling water, blanch the carrots for 5 minutes, then pack them hot inside the jars, leaving a headspace of one inch. If you want a raw pack, place carrots inside

the jar raw, but maintain a headspace of an inch. Ensure the canner is warm, not above a simmer, to prevent a thermal shock. However, the canner should be above and close to boiling if you want a hot pack.

5. Irrespective of the packing technique, pour the boiling water atop the carrots in the jars, leaving a headspace of one inch, then add salt if you prefer it salted (1 teaspoon per quart or half teaspoon per pint).

6. The jars should be sealed using 2-part canning lids, then place the jars inside the pressure canner.

7. Put the lid on the pressure canner, set the temperature to make the pressure canner heat up and allow the steam to vent for ten minutes. Put the canning weight in place and let the canner pressurize.

8. Allow the jars to process for 25 minutes for pints or 30 minutes for quarts. For altitudes above 1,000 ft., you should use 10 pounds of pressure; however, ensure the necessary adjustments are made for higher altitudes. Refer to the section on **Adjusting Altitudes for Home Canning** in chapter 2

9. When the jars have processed, let the pressure canner cool off completely before attempting to open the jars for unloading. (Use your jar lifter for unloading).
10. Check the seals thoroughly. If any jar is unsealed, refrigerate and consume immediately.
11. If your sealed jars are appropriately processed, they will maintain a pantry shelf-life of 1 year-1¹/2 year.
12. Do not forget to strictly abide by the manufacturer's directions as stated in the manual inside your pressure canner. Directions may vary based on your model.

Note

- The quantity of carrots required to pressure a batch depends on the carrots' size, how the carrot's trimming is done, and the chopping size before placing them inside the jars.
- For the quantity yield, a canner batch of 7 quarts requires 16-18 pounds of carrots, and a canner batch of 9 pints requires 10-12 pounds of carrots. A 30-quart all-American Canner can take up to 14 quarts requiring 30-35 pounds of carrots.

Whole Kernel Corn

Ingredients

- 31 ½ lbs. (for 7 quarts) or 20 lbs. (for 9 pints) fresh, in-husk corn
- Salt (optional)

Instructions

1. Prepare your whole kernel corn by husking and desilking the corn, and wash the cob carefully using clean water.
2. Use a knife to cut the corn from the cob and three-fourths depth of the kernel. Avoid scraping the cob.
3. If you want a raw pack, fill up the jars with the corn kernels, leaving sufficient space in case it expands.

4. Add salt if you desire (1 teaspoon per quart or half teaspoon per pint). Then add boiling water, maintaining a headspace of one inch.

5. If you want a hot pack per pint jar, add a cup of water to a pan alongside the prepared corn. Add 2 cups of water for each quart alongside the prepared corn for a quart. Heat the water for 5 minutes and allow it to boil gently. If you desire to add salt, add one teaspoon per quart or half teaspoon per pint. Pour the boiling liquid and corn inside the jars, maintaining a headspace of one inch.

6. Using 2 part canning lids, seal the jars and place them inside the canner.

7. Put the lid on the pressure canner and allow it to boil and the steam to vent for 10 minutes before adding the weight of the pressure canner, allowing it to attain the right temperature. If you use a dial gauge pressure canner at an altitude not more than 2,000 ft., the pressure should be 11 pounds. However, if you use a weighted gauge pressure canner at an altitude not more than 1,000 ft., the pressure should be 10 pounds. Refer to the section on **Adjusting Altitudes for Home Canning** in chapter 2.

8. If you are processing quarts, allow the process to run for 1 hour, 25 minutes, and 55 minutes for pints. When the pressure canner attains the right pressure level, begin the timing.
9. When the processing is complete, allow the pressure canner to completely cool off before you open and unload the jars using a jar lifter.
10. After the jars have cooked off completely, check the seals thoroughly, and if any jar is not sealed properly, refrigerate and consume immediately.
11. You can store the processed jars on a pantry shelf, which is safe between 11-18 months.

Note

1. To make cream-style corn, follow the recipe and use pint or half pint jars. Go through the same preparation process, but you should rather cut the corn kernels in the middle of the kernel. Remove the corn and the corn pulp from the husk using a knife, and add a cup of water per 2 cups of the prepared corn inside a pan. Boil gently, then add a teaspoon of salt for each pint and half a teaspoon for every half pint per jar if you desire to use salt.

2. Pour the liquid and hot corn inside the jars, maintaining a headspace of one inch. Then, with 2-part canning lids, seal the jars, place them inside the pressure canner, and process them for 25 minutes at a pressure of 11 pounds for altitudes less than 2,000 ft. Suppose you use a weighted gauge pressure cooker and process for one hour 25 minutes at a pressure of 10 pounds and an altitude not more than 1,000 ft. Refer to the section on **Adjusting Altitudes for Home Canning** in chapter 2.
3. When the processing is complete, allow the pressure canner to cool off completely before attempting to open the canners to unload the jars using a jar lifter.
4. Check the seals thoroughly, refrigerate any unsealed jar, and consume immediately.

Peas

Ingredients

- Garden Peas (shelled)
- Water

- Salt (this is optional)

Instructions

1. Prepare the peas by shelling and cleaning them if they've not been shelled.
2. Prepare your pressure canner and warm the base of the canner with water (2-3 inches) and heat to a temperature of about 140° F. Always abide by the manufacturer's directions as stated in your pressure canner manual (For either hot pack or raw pack).
3. For the raw pack, heat water (1-1¹/2 cups per pint jar) to boil. Then load the shelled peas inside the pint or quart jars, maintaining a headspace of one inch. Allow the peas to settle, and do not pack the peas down naturally.
4. Use 2 part canning lids to seal the jars tightly and place them inside the pressure canner.

5. Turn up the pressure canner's heat after closing the lid. Then allow the pressure canner to attain boiling point and the steam to vent for 10 minutes. Add the canning weight and pressurize the canner. If you use a weighted gauge pressure canner at an altitude less than 1,000 ft., use a 10 pounds pressure. Refer to the section on **Adjusting Altitudes for Home Canning** in chapter 2.

6. When the canner attains the required pressure, begin the timing (40 minutes) and maintain the pressure. Whatever the elevation and size of the jar, the timing remains unchanged.

7. When the processing is complete, turn off the canner and allow it to cool off to room temperature before removing the weight.

8. Check the sealed jars thoroughly, refrigerate any unsealed jar, and consume immediately. All properly sealed jars have a pantry shelf life of a year and a half.

Note

Peas are vegetables with low acid levels and have to be pressure canned. Water bath canning of peas is improper and unsafe.

Sweet Potatoes

Ingredients

- Sweet Potatoes
- Water
- Sugar (this is optional)

Instructions

1. Prepare the sweet potatoes by washing them, placing them in a pot, and heating them between 15-20 minutes.
2. Turn the heat off and rove the pot allowing it cool until you can handle it.
3. Prepare your pressure canner by warming the base of the canner with water (2-3 inches) and with the trivet in place, then bring to simmer.

4. Prepare a canning syrup or clean water in a separate pot, and allow it to boil.

5. As the pressure canner heats, begin peeling the sweet potatoes using a knife or your fingers. This will be easy since they've been cooked a bit.

6. Cut the sweet potatoes to a regular size and pack them into the jars, maintaining a headspace of one inch. (If the size of your sweet potatoes is small, you may can them in whole).

7. Pour the canning syrup or water over the sweet potatoes inside the canning jars.

8. Remove any air bubbles, adjust the headspace as required, and seal the jars with 2 part canning lids.

9. Place the jars inside the pressure canner and close the lid.

10. Let the steam vent for about 10 minutes and place the canning weight, allowing the canner to pressurize. If you use a weighted gauge pressure canner at sea level, the pressure level should be 10 pounds. Refer to the section on **Adjusting Altitudes for Home Canning** in chapter 2.

11. Allow the canner to process for one hour 30 minutes (quarts) and one hour 5 minutes for pints.

12. When the processing time is complete, turn the heat off and allow the canner to cool off completely.
13. After cooling, open the canners and unload the jars using a jar lifter.
14. Check seals thoroughly; refrigerate if any jar is improperly sealed, and consume immediately.
15. All properly canned and sealed jars have a pantry shelf-life between 12-18 months.

Note

- Regarding the quantity yield, the efficiency of your peeling and the size of the sweet potatoes will determine the quantity needed. However, 7 quarts will require 14-16 pounds of sweet potatoes, and a 9 pint will require 9-19 pounds of sweet potatoes.
- Your sweet potatoes can be pressure canned in water or syrup of any texture. Preferably, use extra light syrup for the preservation of the natural taste.
- If you want to prepare an extra light syrup, for a 9-pint batch, mid $6^1/2$ cups of water and $^3/4$ cups of sugar. For a 7-quart batch, mix 10 $^1/2$ cups of water and $1^1/4$ cups of sugar.

Pumpkin

Ingredients

- Pumpkin
- Water

Instructions

1. Prepare the pumpkins by removing the seeds and strings and slicing them up in half sizes. Slice the half pumpkins into inch strips, then chop them into inch cubes; then, with a paring knife, slice each peeled cube or peel the inch slice before they are chopped into cubes.
2. Prepare your pressure canner and the jars.

3. Boil water in a large pot and add the pumpkins, then allow to cook for 2 minutes until it is properly heated. However, do not overcook to avoid the chunks falling apart.
4. Scoop chunks of the pumpkin with a slotted spoon into the jars and add the blanched water maintaining a headspace of one inch.
5. Remove air bubbles from the jar, adjust the headspace as needed, and use 2 part canning lids to seal.
6. Place the jars into the pressure canner and close the lid.
7. Turn up the heat, allow the steam to vent for about 10 minutes, and place the canning weight.
8. Bring the pressure canner up to 10 pounds pressure. Refer to the section on **Adjusting Altitudes for Home Canning** in chapter 2.
9. Process the jars for 55 minutes for pints and one hour 30 minutes for quarts.
10. When the processing time is complete, turn the heat off and allow the pressure canner to cool off to room temperature.
11. Open the canner, unload the jars using a jar lifter, and check the seals thoroughly. If any jar is improperly sealed, refrigerate and consume immediately.

12. All jars adequately canned and sealed maintain quality with a pantry shelf-life between 12-18 months.

Note

For quantity yield, a 7-quart batch will require 16-20 pounds (approximately 2¼ -3 pounds for each quart jar). A pumpkin cube takes about 1½-¾ pound for each pint jar.

Mushrooms

Ingredients

- Brightly colored mushrooms of 14½ pounds (for 9 pints) or 7½ pounds (for nine half pints, averagely 2 pounds per pint)
- Salt (this is optional)
- Ascorbic acid or 500mg vitamin C tablet (for better color)

Instructions

1. Prepare the mushrooms by trimming the stems and discolored parts, then soak in cold water for 10 minutes to remove the specks of dirt.
2. Wash the mushrooms in clean water.
3. Cut the large mushrooms to the desired size, leaving the small ones whole.
4. Prepare your pressure canner and the jars.
5. For a hot pack, pour the mushrooms into a saucepan and boil for 5 minutes.
6. Fill up the jars with the mushrooms maintaining a headspace of one inch.
7. Pour clean water into a separate pot and allow to boil.
8. If you desire, add salt (½ teaspoon per pint).
9. For a nice coloration, add 1/8 ascorbic acid powder or a 500mg vitamin C tablet.

10. Place the jars inside the pressure canner, pour the boiled water into it, and close the lid.
11. Turn up the heat and allow the steam to vent for about 10 minutes before placing the canning weight.
12. Bring the pressure of the canner to 11 pounds at an altitude not more than 2,000 ft., and if you are using a weighted gauge pressure canner, a pressure of 10 pounds at an altitude not greater than 1,000 ft. Refer to the section on **Adjusting Altitudes for Home Canning** in chapter 2.
13. Allow the pressure canner to process for 45 minutes (for pints).
14. When the processing time is complete, turn off the heat and allow the pressure canner to cool off to room temperature.
15. Open the canner, unload the jars using a jar lifter, and check the seals thoroughly. If any jar is improperly sealed, refrigerate and consume immediately.
16. All adequately canned and sealed jars maintain quality with a pantry shelf-life between 12-18 months.

Okra

Ingredients

- Okra 26 pounds (a bushel) fir 16-18 quarts.
- Salt (this is optional).

Instructions

1. Prepare the okra by washing the pods and trimming the ends.
2. You may leave the okra whole or cut them into pieces and pour them into a saucepan. Pour clean water and allow to boil for 2 minute
3. Drain the water from the saucepan
4. Prepare your pressure canner and the jars.

5. For a hot pack, fill up the prepared jars with hot okra and maintain a headspace of one inch.
6. Remove air bubbles from the jar, adjust the headspace as needed, and use 2 part canning lids to seal.
7. If you desire to use salt, add ½ teaspoon to the pint jars or one teaspoon per quart.
8. Pour clean water into a separate pot and allow to boil.
9. Fill up the jars with the prepared okra maintaining a headspace of one inch.
10. Remove air bubbles from the jar, adjust the headspace as needed, and use 2 part canning lids to seal.
11. Place the jars inside the pressure canner, pour the boiled water, and then close the lid.
12. Turn up the heat and allow the steam to vent for about 10 minutes before placing the canning weight.
13. Bring the pressure of the canner to 11 pounds pressure at an altitude not more than 2,000 feet and 10 pounds pressure at an altitude no greater than 1,000 ft. if you are using a weighted gauge pressure canner. Refer to the section on **Adjusting Altitudes for Home Canning** in chapter 2.

14. Allow the pressure canner to process for 25 minutes (for pints).
15. When the processing time is complete, turn off the heat and allow the pressure canner to cool off at room temperature.
16. Open the canner, unload the jars using a jar lifter, and check the seals thoroughly. If any jar is improperly sealed, refrigerate and consume immediately.
17. All adequately canned and sealed jars maintain quality with a pantry shelf-life between 12-18 months.

Note

For the quantity yield, 7 quarts require 11-12 pounds of okra and 7-8 pounds for 9 pints. A bushel (26 pounds) will yield 16-18 quarts (averagely 1½ pounds per quart).

Chapter 7

Recipes for Meat, Poultry, and Seafood

Chicken

Ingredients

- Boned or boneless chicken (for whole, cut in smaller sizes or use particular parts).
- Salt (this is optional).

Instructions

1. Prepare your pressure canner and the jars.
2. Prepare your chicken. If your chicken is with bones, cut the meats at the joints and ensure the

cut pieces can enter your jars. If your chicken is without bones, cut them into desired sizes.

3. For a raw pack, place the chickens inside the jars. (You can sprinkle the cut chicken pieces with pepper, salt, and garlic powder if you desire before packing them inside the jars. This is for flavor and taste but optional).

4. Fill up your jars with the chicken pieces and add salt or any other ingredients you might wish to add. ($1/2$ teaspoon of salt per pint jar, and one teaspoon per quart jar.)

5. Fill the jars with clean hot water or broth, maintaining a headspace of one inch.

6. For a hot pack, after cutting up the chicken to desired sizes, boil it and allow it to steam to the point of being two-thirds cooked.

7. Fill up the jars with the chicken pieces and add salt if desired. ($1/2$ teaspoon per pint jar, and one teaspoon per quart jar.)

8. Fill the jars with clean hot water or broth, maintaining a headspace of one inch.

9. Get rid of the air bubbles with a knife or canning tool.

10. Clean the rims, adjust the lids, and place them inside your pressure canner.

11. If you are canning chicken with no bones, process the jars for one hour, 5 minutes for pints, and one hour for thirty minutes for quarts. Suppose you are canning chicken with bones, process for one hour, five minutes for pints, and one hour for fifteen minutes for quarts. The processing time does not change for raw or hot packs.

12. If you are using a dial gauge pressure canner, you should process the jars at a pressure of 11 lbs. for altitudes not more than 2,000 ft. If you use a weighted gauge pressure canner, process the jars at a pressure of 10 lbs. for altitudes not more than 1,000 ft. Check altitude adjustment tables in the previous chapters for the necessary adjustments.

Turkey

Ingredients

- Turkey (stock or thawed)
- Salt (this is optional)

Instructions

1. Prepare the turkey by cooking it slightly and heating the oven to 350° F.
2. Place the turkey directly in a roasting pan with the breast facing upwards
3. Remove the turkey's neck, the giblets from the neck, the main body, and the base of the roasting pan around the turkey.
4. Add water to the pan (2-3 cups), cove, and roast the turkey to the point of being two-thirds cooked. This is attained at a temperature measurement of 120° F on a thermometer. (About 3 hours). If you prefer to fully cook your turkey, heat it to 165° F.
5. Allow the turkey to cool off completely. Separate the meat from the bones, and cut it to desired sizes.
6. Prepare your pressure canner and the jars.

7. Fill up the jars with water after placing them inside the pressure canner. Always follow the manufacturer's directions when canning.

8. Fill up the jar rack with hot water, and put them inside the pressure canner using a jar lifter. Heat the canner to 180° F and allow to simmer for 10 minutes. Maintain the temperature until you are ready to process the turkey.

9. Using your jar lifter, remove the jar and empty the water. Place the jar on your kitchen towel and fill up the jar with the meat maintaining a headspace of one inch at the jar's top. Then add salt if you desire. (1 teaspoon for a quart and 1/2 teaspoon for a pint.) Fill up the jar and cover it, maintaining a headspace of one inch.

10. Remove air bubbles from the jars, and clean the rim. Then screw your jars tightly.

11. Put the jars back inside the pressure canner, and repeat the process until all your turkey is inside the jars in the pressure canner.

12. Place the canner lid and cover appropriately. Increase the heat to a high temperature for a boil, and allow the steam to vent for about 10 minutes before placing the canner weight.

13. If you use a weighted gauge pressure canner, allow the canner to reach a pressure of 10 pounds

and 11 pounds if you use a dial gauge pressure canner. Allow the jars to process for one hour, 15 minutes (for pints), and one and a half hours (for quarts) for altitudes not more than 1,000 ft.

14. Make the necessary heat adjustments to maintain the pressure. Check altitude adjustment tables in the previous chapters for the necessary adjustments.

15. After the processing time has elapsed, turn the heat off, and allow the pressure canner to cool off completely.

16. When it is cooled off, unlock the cover and use a jar lifter to remove all jars from your pressure canner.

17. Check the seals thoroughly, and if there is any improperly sealed jar, refrigerate it and consume it immediately.

18. Store all properly canned and sealed jars on a pantry shelf. The quality is maintained between 12-18 months.

Beef

Ingredients

- Grounded beef or cubed chunks of beef
- Water, tomato juice, or broth

Instructions

1. Prepare your pressure canner based on the manufacturer's manual.
2. Prepare your beef by removing fat as much as possible and browning the meat. (Either grounded or chunks.)
3. While you brown the meat, heat clean water (you can also use tomato juice or broth) and allow it to boil.
4. Fill up the jars with the browned beef while maintaining a headspace of one inch.

5. With a 2-part canning lid, seal the jars after cleaning the rims.
6. Place the jars inside your pressure canner that has been heated, cover the lid and let the steam vent for 10 minutes.
7. Place the canning weight, and allow the pressure canner to pressurize.
8. When the pressure canner attains the required pressure, let the jars process for one hour, 15 minutes (pints), and one and a half hours (quarts).
9. After the processing, turn the heat off, allowing the pressure canner to cool off to room temperature. Then unseal the pressure canner and unload the jars.
10. Check the seals thoroughly, immediately consume any improperly sealed jars, and store up properly canned and sealed jars on a pantry shelf. You can maintain the quality of the processed jars between 12-18 months.

Note

1. Do not water bath can the beef. Rather, pressure can.

2. The preparation procedures are the same whether you are pressure canning a chunk of ground beef.
3. For recipe yield, it takes approximately 3/4 lbs. raw beef to fill a pint and 1¹/2 lbs. raw beef to fill a quart. These size measurements apply to any pressure canning methods you may want.
4. If you see fat at the top of your jars after pressure canning, that is not a problem, and this is most common with hamburgers and ground beef. When you brown the meat, ensure to remove fat from the meat to avoid excess fat after processing your beef. However, if you notice a solid fat at the top of your jar, that is not a problem. It depends on the beef used for the canning. If the fat is in excess, it can bubble up when pressure canning, and if the fat gets into the seal, it can prevent the jars from sealing. This is simpler than canning beef if you are pressure canning a beef broth. Prepare the broth, filtering out the solids. Then return the stock to a boiling temperature and ladle it into the jars, maintaining a headspace of one inch. The processing time for just the broth is lesser (20 minutes for pints and 25 minutes for quarts.)
5. The altitude adjustments for beef chunks or ground beef are not different. However, the

pressure differs slightly based on your pressure canner's model. Check the altitude adjustments table from previous chapters for the necessary adjustments.

Mincemeat Pie Filling

Ingredients

- One lb. of white raisins
- Two tablespoons of salt
- Two tablespoons of ground cinnamon
- Two teaspoons of grounded nutmeg
- Two cups of chopped suet
- Two qts. of apple cider
- Two lbs. of dark raisins (seedless)
- Four lbs. of ground beef (another option is 4 lbs. of ground venison and one lb. sausage.)
- Five cups of sugar
- Five qts chopped apples

Recipe yield: 7 quarts

Instructions

1. Prepare your pressure canner and jars based on the manufacturer's directions.
2. Peel, core, and quarter your apples.
3. Cook the meat and suet in clean water to prevent browning.
4. Grind the suet, apples, and meat using a medium-sized blade food grinder.
5. Using a big saucepan, add all the ingredients and simmer them for an hour until they thicken. Stir the mixture properly.
6. Fill up the jars with the mixture, maintaining a headspace of one inch.
7. Adjust the lids and seal properly, placing the jars into your pressure canner using a jar lifter.

8. If you are using a dial gauge pressure canner, allow your mincemeat pie to process for one and a half hours (quarts) at a pressure of 11 lbs. for altitudes not more than 2,000 ft. However, if you use a weighted gauge pressure canner, allow the mincemeat pie to process for one and a half hours (quarts) at a pressure of 10 lbs. for altitudes not more than 1,000 ft. and 15lbs. for altitudes above 1,000 ft. Check the altitude adjustments table from previous chapters for the necessary adjustments.
9. After the processing time has elapsed, turn the heat off, and allow the pressure canner to cool off completely.
10. When it is cooled off, unlock the cover and use a jar lifter to remove all jars from your pressure canner.
11. Check the seals thoroughly, and if there is any improperly sealed jar, refrigerate it and consume it immediately.
12. Store all properly canned and sealed jars on a pantry shelf. The quality is maintained between 12-18 months.

Venison, Elk, Moose, and Caribou

Ingredients

- Venison, Elk, Moose, or Caribou
- Onion (a large one diced in small sizes.)
- Green pepper (one large size that is well seeded and diced in small sizes.)
- One teaspoon of grounded black pepper
- Two teaspoons of salt
- Two tablespoons of canning gel (use a modified corn starch safe for canning.)
- Two-Four tablespoons of extra virgin olive oil
- Six minced garlic cloves.
- Vegetables (chopped)
- Seasonings

Instructions

1. Prepare your pressure canner and jars based on the manufacturer's directions.
2. Prepare your meat by trimming it free of excessive fat, gristle, bruised spots, and silver skin.
3. Cut your meat to the desired size of cubes, strips, or chunks. (Preferably 1 or 2 inches.)
4. Dry the meat using a paper towel for proper browning.
5. Brown all sides of the meat in batches with one tablespoon of olive oil per batch in a stock pot of medium size.
6. While browning the meat, avoid cooking it and use the delicious drippings for future use. Remove the browned meat from the stock pot and place it in a separate large bowl.
7. Add 2 cups of hot water to the leftover drippings in the stock pot. Whisk in the canning gel and boil the mixture for 2 minutes while often stirring. Remove the mixture from the heat after boiling for 2 minutes.
8. Add the minced garlic cloves, seasonings, and chopped vegetables to the browned meat in the bowl and mix properly using your hands (wear

plastic gloves). This will enable the coating of the meat with the added ingredients.

9. Fill up jars with the mixed meat while maintaining a headspace of one inch. Then spoon the hot broth from the drippings over the meat while maintaining the headspace of one inch.

10. Remove the air bubbles using your canning tool and adjust the headspace.

11. Wipe the rims clean using a kitchen cloth, and tighten the lids.

12. Place your jars inside the pressure canner using a jar lifter.

13. Process the jars for one hour 15 minutes (pints) at a pressure of 10 lbs. and one hour 30 minutes (quarts). Check the altitude adjustments table from previous chapters for the necessary adjustments.

13. After the processing time has elapsed, turn the heat off, and allow the pressure canner to cool off completely.

14. When it is cooled off, unlock the cover and use a jar lifter to remove all jars from your pressure canner.

15. Check the seals thoroughly, and if there is any improperly sealed jar, refrigerate it and consume it immediately.

16. Store all properly canned and sealed jars on a pantry shelf. The quality is maintained between 12-18 months.

Clams

Ingredients

- Clams
- Two tablespoons of lemon juice or $1/2$ teaspoon of Citric acid.
- One teaspoon of salt per quart.

Instructions

1. Prepare your pressure canner and jars based on the manufacturer's instructions.

2. Get the clams ready by keeping them on ice till you are ready for canning.
3. Thoroughly scrub the shells, rinse with water, and then steam for 5 minutes.
4. Open the clams and bring out the meat. Gather and save the juice from the clam.
5. Wash the clam meat thoroughly in clean water with one teaspoon of salt for each quart
6. Use boiling water to rinse and cover the clam meat with two tablespoons of lemon juice or half a teaspoon of citric acid per gallon inside boiling water, then allow it to boil for 2 minutes before draining.
7. If you prefer minced clams, use a food processor to grind the clams.
8. Fill up the jars with pieces of clam meats, and add the hot juice from the clam saved initially with water (boiled) if needed. Maintain a headspace of one inch at the top of the jars.
9. Remove the air bubbles using your canning tool and adjust the headspace.
10. Wipe the rims clean using a kitchen cloth, and tighten the lids.
11. Place your jars inside the pressure canner using a jar lifter. If you use a dial gauge pressure canner, process the jars for 1 hour 10 minutes (pints) or 1

hour (half pints) at a pressure of 11 lbs. for altitudes not more than 2,000 ft. However, if you use a weighted gauge pressure canner, process the jars for 1 hour 10 minutes (pints) or 1 hour for (half pints) at a pressure of 10 lbs. for altitudes not more than 1,000 ft. Check the altitude adjustments table from previous chapters for the necessary adjustments.

12. After the processing time has elapsed, turn the heat off, and allow the pressure canner to cool off completely.

13. When it is cooled off, unlock the cover and use a jar lifter to remove all jars from your pressure canner.

14. Check the seals thoroughly, and if there is any improperly sealed jar, refrigerate it and consume it immediately.

King and Dungeness Crab Meat

Ingredients

- Crab
- Quarter cup of lemon juice or citric acid.

- Four cups of white vinegar
- Two tablespoons of salt

Instructions

1. Prepare your pressure canner and jars based on the manufacturer's instructions.
2. Begin the preparation of the crab by keeping them live on ice until you are ready for canning.
3. Thoroughly wash the crabs several times using cold water.
4. Add two tablespoons of salt or 1/4 cup of lemon juice to the water and use it to simmer the crabs for about 20 minutes.
5. Remove the crabs' shell, and separate the meat from the body and claws.
6. Add 4 cups of white vinegar or 2 cups of lemon juice and two tablespoons of salt in cold water

and soak the crab meat for 2 minutes. Then drain the crab meat from moisture.

7. Fill up your half-pint jars with 6 ounces of crab meat and pint jars with 12 ounces of crab meat while maintaining a headspace of one inch.

8. Add two tablespoons per half-pint jar and four tablespoons of lemon juice to each pint jar. Then add hot water while maintaining a headspace of one inch.

9. Remove the air bubbles using your canning tool and adjust the headspace.

10. Wipe the rims clean using a kitchen cloth, and tighten the lids.

11. Place your jars inside the pressure canner using a jar lifter.

12. Process the jars according to the altitude adjustments table shown below.

13. After the processing time has elapsed, turn the heat off, and allow the pressure canner to cool off completely.

14. When it is cooled off, unlock the cover and use a jar lifter to remove all jars from your pressure canner.

15. Check the seals thoroughly, and if there is any improperly sealed jar, refrigerate it and consume it immediately.

16. Store all properly canned and sealed jars on a pantry shelf. The quality is maintained between 12-18 months.

Table 1. Recommended process time for **King and Dungeness Crab Meat** in a dial-gauge pressure canner.

Jar Size	Process Time	Canner Pressure (PSI) at Altitudes of			
		0 - 2,000 ft	2,001 - 4,000 ft	4,001 - 6,000 ft	6,001 - 8,000 ft
Half-pints	70 min	11 lb	12 lb	13 lb	14 lb
Pints	80	11	12	13	14

Table 2. Recommended process time for **King and Dungeness Crab Meat** in a weighted-gauge pressure canner.

Jar Size	Process Time	Canner Pressure (PSI) at Altitudes of	
		0 - 1,00 ft	Above 1,000 ft
Half-pints	70 min	10 lb	15 lb
Pints	80	10	15

Note

For best quality, it is suggested that blue crab meat should be frozen rather than canned. If crab meat is canned based on the instructions given above, the crab meat may have a specific flavor that is acidic. In light of this, freezing is the recommended preservation method.

Fish

Ingredients

- Fish (Blue, Trout, Mackerel, Steelhead, Salmon, and other Fatty Fish Excluding Tuna)
- Salt (this is optional)

Instructions

1. Prepare your pressure canner and jars based on the manufacturer's instructions.
2. Keep the fish on ice until you are ready for canning.
3. Prepare your fish by removing the fins, scales, tail, and head.
4. Wash the skin thoroughly, and remove the blood.

5. Cut the fish into the desired size (3- ½ inches lengths).
6. Fill up the jars with the fish, placing the skin portion next to the glass. Maintain a headspace of one inch.
7. Add a teaspoon of salt to each pint (this is optional.)
8. You should not add liquids or fluids to the jars.
9. Wipe the rims clean using a kitchen cloth, and tighten the lids.
10. Place your jars inside the pressure canner using a jar lifter.
11. If you use a dial gauge pressure canner, process the jars for 100 minutes (pints) at a pressure of 11 lbs. for altitudes not more than 2,000 ft. However, if you use a weighted gauge pressure canner, process the jars for 100 minutes at a pressure of 10 lbs. for altitudes not more than 1,000 ft. Check the altitude table below for more information.
12. After the processing time has elapsed, turn the heat off, and allow the pressure canner to cool off completely.
13. When it is cooled off, unlock the cover and use a jar lifter to remove all jars from your pressure canner.

14. Check the seals thoroughly, and if there is any improperly sealed jar, refrigerate it and consume it immediately.

15. Store up all properly canned and sealed jars; the quality is maintained between 12-18 months.

Table 1. Recommended process time for **Fish** in a dial-gauge pressure canner.

Style of Pack	Jar Size	Process Time	Canner Pressure (PSI) at Altitudes of			
			0 - 2,000 ft	2,001 - 4,000 ft	4,001 - 6,000 ft	6,001 - 8,000 ft
Raw	Pints	100 min	11 lb	12 lb	13 lb	14 lb

Table 2. Recommended process time for **Fish** in a weighted-gauge pressure canner.

Style of Pack	Jar Size	Process Time	Canner Pressure (PSI) at Altitudes of	
			0 - 1,000 ft	Above 1,000 ft
Raw	Pints	100 min	10 lb	15 lb

Note

When salmons are pressure canned, crystals like a glass of magnesium ammonium phosphate usually form in the jars. Home Canning cannot prevent the formation of crystals. However, the crystals will dissolve when they pass through heat and are safe for consumption.

Oysters

Ingredients

- Oysters
- Salt

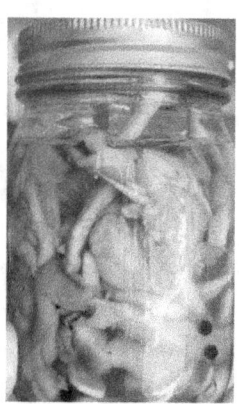

Instructions

1. Prepare your pressure canner and jars based on the manufacturer's directions.
2. Ensure you keep the oysters on ice until you are ready for canning.
3. Prepare your oysters by washing the shells and heating them at a temperature of 400° F in a preheated oven.

4. Allow the oysters to cool slightly in ice water, then drain and separate the shells from the meat.

5. Wash the meat thoroughly in water with a half cup of salt for each gallon, then drain.

6. Fill up your jars (half pints or pints), then add half a teaspoon of salt per pint if desired. Fill the jars with hot water while maintaining a headspace of one inch.

7. Wipe the rims clean using a kitchen cloth, and tighten the lids.

8. Place your jars inside the pressure canner using a jar lifter.

9. If you use a dial gauge pressure canner, process the jars for 1 hour 15 minutes (half pints or pints) at a pressure of 11 lbs. for altitudes not more than 2,000 ft. However, if you use a weighted gauge pressure canner, process the jars for 1 hour 15 minutes at a pressure of 10 lbs. for altitudes not more than 1,000 ft. Check the altitude table below for more information.

10. After the processing time is complete, turn the heat off, and allow the pressure canner to cool off completely.

11. When it is cooled off, unlock the cover and use a jar lifter to remove all jars from your pressure canner.

12. Check the seals thoroughly, and if there is any improperly sealed jar, refrigerate it and consume it immediately.
13. Store up all properly canned and sealed jars. The quality is maintained between 12-18 months.

Table 1. Recommended process time for **Oysters** in a dial-gauge pressure canner.

Jar Size	Process Time	Canner Pressure (PSI) at Altitudes of			
		0 - 2,000 ft	2,001 - 4,000 ft	4,001 - 6,000 ft	6,001 - 8,000 ft
Half-pints or Pints	75 min	**11 lb**	12 lb	13 lb	14 lb

Table 2. Recommended process time for **Oysters** in a weighted-gauge pressure canner.

Jar Size	Process Time	Canner Pressure (PSI) at Altitudes of	
		0 - 1,000 ft	Above 1,000 ft
Half-pints or Pints	75 min	**10 lb**	15 lb

Tuna

Ingredients

- Tuna
- Water or oil
- Salt

Instructions

1. Prepare your pressure canner based on the manufacturer's instructions.
2. Ensure to keep the tuna iced until you are ready for canning.
3. Wash the fish properly in cold water and remove the viscera.
4. Wash and drain blood from the skin, and put the belly on a metal tray on the base of a baking pan.
5. Cut the tuna to moderate size as desired.
6. At a temperature of 250° F, preheat the fish between $2^{1}/2 - 4$ hours or 350° F for an hour based on the tuna size. Alternatively, cook the tuna using a steamer for 2-4 hours.

7. Then refrigerate the cooked fish between 6-12 hours to make the tuna firm.
8. Use a knife to peel off the skin, separate the meat from bones, and remove discolored flesh.
9. Cut out and remove all bones, fins, and dark flesh.
10. Fill up the jars with tuna gently after cutting into quarters, then pour oil or water, maintaining a headspace of one inch.
11. Add half a teaspoon of salt for each half pint and one teaspoon for each pint (this is optional)
12. Wipe the rims clean using a kitchen cloth, and tighten the lids.
13. Place your jars inside the pressure canner using a jar lifter.
14. If you use a dial gauge pressure canner, process the jars for 100 minutes (half pints or pints) at a pressure of 11 lbs. for altitudes not more than 2,000 ft. However, if you use a weighted gauge pressure canner, process the jars for 1 hour 100 minutes at a pressure of 10 lbs. for altitudes not more than 1,000 ft. Check the altitude table below for more information.
15. After the processing time is complete, turn the heat off, and allow the pressure canner to cool off completely.

16. When it is cooled off, unlock the cover and use a jar lifter to remove all jars from your pressure canner.
17. Check the seals thoroughly, and if there is any improperly sealed jar, refrigerate it and consume it immediately.
18. Store up all properly canned and sealed jars. The quality is maintained between 12-18 months.

Table 1. Recommended process time for **Tuna** in a dial-gauge pressure canner.

Jar Size	Process Time	Canner Pressure (PSI) at Altitudes of			
		0 - 2,000 ft	2,001 - 4,000 ft	4,001 - 6,000 ft	6,001 - 8,000 ft
Pints and Half-pints	100 min	**11 lb**	12 lb	13 lb	14 lb

Table 2. Recommended process time for **Tuna** in a weighted-gauge pressure canner.

Jar Size	Process Time	Canner Pressure (PSI) at Altitudes of	
		0 - 1,000 ft	Above 1,000 ft
Pints and Half-pints	100 min	**10 lb**	15 lb

Note

Tuna pressure canned raw or preheated. When they are preheated, it removes the strong flavor of the oils, mostly. When tunas are pressure canned, crystals like a glass of magnesium ammonium phosphate usually form in the jars. Home Canning cannot prevent the formation of crystals. However, the crystals will

116

dissolve when they pass through heat and are safe for consumption.

The end... almost!

Hey! We've made it to the final chapter of this book, and I hope you've enjoyed it so far.

If you have not done so yet, I would be incredibly thankful if you could take just a minute to leave a quick review on Amazon

Reviews are not easy to come by, and as an independent author with a little marketing budget, I rely on you, my readers, to leave a short review on Amazon.

Even if it is just a sentence or two!

So if you really enjoyed this book, please...

>> Click here to leave a brief review on Amazon.

I truly appreciate your effort to leave your review, as it truly makes a huge difference.

Chapter 8

Recipes for Soups, Stocks, and Broths

Vegetable Soup

Ingredients

- Two cups of chopped onions (medium size)
- Two cups of 1 inch sliced celery (4 stalks)
- Four cups of raw corn kernels
- Four cups of green lima beans (1-1/2 pounds)
- Six cups of water
- Six cups of potatoes (peeled and cubed)
- Six cups of water
- Eight cups of tomatoes (peeled, chopped, and cored between 4-12 lbs.)
- Salt (this is optional)
- Pepper (this is optional)

Recipe yield: Between 6-8 quarts (32 oz)

Instructions

1. Prepare your pressure canner and jars based on the manufacturer's directions.
2. Mix the vegetables in a big pot, add water and allow it to boil.
3. When it boils, reduce the heat and allow it to simmer for 5 minutes.
4. Season it using salt and pepper (this is optional).
5. Scoop the hot soup into the prepared jars, leaving a headspace of one inch.
6. Remove air bubbles using your canning tool.
7. Wipe the rim clean with a kitchen cloth, and seal the lids tightly.

8. With a jar lifter, place your jars into the pressure canner.
9. Process the jar at a pressure of 10 pounds for 55 minutes (pints), and 85 minutes (quarts), adjust the altitude as necessary.
10. After the processing time is complete, turn off the heat and allow the canner to cool off completely.
11. Remove the processed jars from the canner and check the lids thoroughly.
12. If any jar is not properly sealed, refrigerate and consume immediately.

Chicken Soup

Ingredients

- One cup of diced onions
- Half-One cup of carrots (sliced)
- Half-One cup of celery
- Three cups of cooked chicken (diced)
- Three cups of diced
- Three cubes of chicken bouillon
- Sixteen cups of chicken stock

- Pepper (this is optional)
- Salt (this is optional)

Recipe yield: Between 2-4 quart jars or 3-8 pint jars

Instructions

1. Prepare your pressure canner and jars based on the manufacturer's instructions.
2. Mix the chicken stock, carrots, chicken, celery, and onion in a big stock pot.
3. Turn on the heat and boil the mixture.
4. When the mixture boils, reduced the heat and simmer for up to half an hour.
5. Add pepper, bouillon cubes and salt if you desire. Then cook until the bouillon cubes dissolved.
6. Pour the chicken soup into the jars, maintaining a headspace of one inch.

7. Remove air bubbles from the jars, and tighten the lid.
8. With a jar lifter, place your jars into the pressure canner.
9. Process the jar at a pressure of 10 pounds for 1 hour 15 minutes (pints), and one hour 30 minutes (quarts), adjust the altitude as necessary.
10. After the processing time is complete, turn off the heat and allow the canner to cool off completely.
11. Remove the processed jars from the canner and check the lids thoroughly.
12. If any jar is not properly sealed, refrigerate and consume immediately.

Split Pea and Ham Soup

Ingredients

- One cup of ham (diced)
- One cup of onion (chopped)
- One and a half cup of carrots (sliced)
- One bay leaf
- Quarter teaspoon of ground allspice

- Two cups of dried split peas
- Two cubes of chicken bouillon
- Eight cups of water
- Salt (this is optional)
- Pepper (this is optional)

Instructions

1. Prepare your pressure canner and jars according to the manufacturer's manual.
2. Add your clean water, bouillon cubes, and split peas in a big soup pot.
3. Boil the mixture in the soup pot, and stir often.
4. Reduce the heat when it boils and allow it to simmer.
5. Allow the peas to cook for one hour so that the peas will become soft.

6. After the peas are cooked, puree the liquid and peas with a food processor.
7. Pour in the onion, carrots, ham, bay leaf, and allspice to the soup and boil.
8. When the soup boils, reduce the heat and allow it to cook for 30 minutes.
9. Add pepper and salt for taste; if the soup is thicker than you want, add little hot water to thin.
10. Stir the soup often, then remove the bay leaf.
11. Pour the soup inside the jar, maintaining a headspace of one inch.
12. Remove air bubbles from the jars, and tighten the lid.
13. With a jar lifter, place your jars into the pressure canner, then turn on the heat to medium, and allow the steam to vent for 10 minutes.
14. Process the jar at a pressure of 10 pounds for 1 hour 15 minutes (pints), and one hour 30 minutes (quarts), adjust the altitude as necessary.
15. After the processing time is complete, turn off the heat and allow the canner to cool off completely.
16. Remove the processed jars from the canner and check the lids thoroughly.

17. If any jar is not properly sealed, refrigerate and consume immediately.

Beef Broth Soup

Ingredients

- One head of garlic (cut into two, do not remove the skin)
- Two gallons of water (or sufficient water for the soup)
- One teaspoon of thyme
- One teaspoon of dried rosemary
- One teaspoon of parsley (dried)
- Three bay leaves.
- Three celery ribs (chopped)
- Three-Four onions (quartered with skins)
- Four-Five carrots (chopped)
- Five-Six pounds of beef stock bones
- Ten peppercorns (whole)

Instructions

1. Prepare your pressure canner and jars based on the manufacturer's instructions.
2. Heat up your oven to a temperature of 450° F.
3. Roast your beef bones in a roasting pan for 45 minutes.
4. Pour the beef bones into a big stockpot and scrape the leftovers from the roasting pan, add water then pour the contents inside the stockpot
5. Add vegetables and aromatics to the stockpot, then pour water (about 2")
6. Boil the broth and allow it to simmer between 4-24 hours.
7. When the broth is cooked, put a colander in line with cheesecloth over another stockpot, pouring the broth into the colander allowing the liquid through to the other stockpot.

8. Carefully pour the broth inside your jars using a canning funnel, and maintain a headspace of one inch.

9. Remove air bubbles from the jars, and tighten the lid.

10. With a jar lifter, place your jars into the pressure canner then turn on the heat to medium, and allow the steam to vent for 10 minutes.

11. If you are using a dial gauge canner, process the jars at a pressure of 11 pounds for 20 minutes (pints), and 25 minutes (quarts). If you use a weighted gauge canner, process the jars at a pressure of 10 pounds for 20 minutes (pints) or 25 minutes (quarts). Refer to the previous chapters on adjusting altitudes for more information.

12. After the processing time is complete, turn off the heat and allow the canner to cool off completely.

13. Remove the processed jars from the canner and check the lids thoroughly.

14. If any jar is not properly sealed, refrigerate and consume immediately.

15. Properly canned and sealed jars can be stored on the shelf between 12-18 months.

Creamy Mushroom Soup

Ingredients

- One teaspoon of ground black pepper
- One tablespoon of arrowroot (flour is another alternative.)
- Quarter cup of cream (heavy)
- Two-third cup of white wine
- Thin sliced mushrooms (2 pounds)
- Two teaspoons of thyme (dried)
- Two tablespoons of butter
- Four teaspoons of salt
- Six garlic cloves (minced)
- Six cups of broth (beef or chicken)
- Eight cups of onions (minced)

Instructions

1. Prepare your pressure canner according to the manufacturer's directions.
2. Melt the butter in a big stockpot, then sauté the garlic and onions on medium heat for 15 minutes or until the onions become translucent.
3. Add the broth, mushrooms, spices, and wine to the stockpot, and boil for 5 minutes on medium-high heat.
4. Turn off the heat and pour the soup into the jars, maintaining a headspace of one inch.
5. Remove air bubbles from the jars using your canning tool while maintaining the headspace. Then wipe the rims clean with a kitchen cloth, and seal the jars tightly.
6. Load your jars into the pressure canner using a jar lifter.
7. Process the jars at a pressure of 10 pounds for 45 minutes (pints), and make necessary adjustments to the altitude. The pressure canning is done in pints because there are no recommendations for canning in quarts.

8. When the processing time is complete, allow the canner to depressurize, then unload the jars from the canner.
9. Check the seals thoroughly; if any jar is not sealed properly, refrigerate and consume immediately.
10. Properly canned and sealed jars can be stored for 12 months.

Meat Bone Broth

Ingredients

- Two onions
- Two cloves of garlic (minced)
- Rosemary sprigs
- Parsley sprigs
- Oregano sprigs
- Bones and carcasses (from poultry, beef, or pork)
- Salt (this is optional)
- Pepper (this is optional)

Instructions

1. Prepare your pressure canner based on the manufacturer's directions.
2. Prepare the bones or carcasses by placing them in the base of a big slow cooker and filling up with water.
3. Add the parsley, celery, onions, oregano, cloves of minced garlic, rosemary, pepper, salt, carrots, and seasonings of your preference.
4. Cover and heat the slow cooker between 12-24 hours.
5. When it is cooked, strain and allow it to cool.
6. Refrigerate the bone broth overnight.

7. Remove any accumulated fat on the bone broth overnight to avoid bad flavoring.
8. Pour the bone broth into a pot and boil.
9. Fill the jars with the bone broth, maintaining a headspace of one inch and seal the jars tightly.
10. Load your jars inside the pressure canner, close the lid and heat it.
11. Process the jars at a pressure of 10 pounds for 20 minutes (pints), and 25 minutes for quarts and adjust for altitudes.
12. When the processing time is complete, turn off the heat and allow the pressure canner to depressurize completely.
13. Unload your jars from the pressure canner and check the seals thoroughly. If any jar is not properly sealed, refrigerate and consume immediately.
14. Properly canned and sealed jars can be stored for 12 months.

Chicken Stock

Ingredients

- Chicken bones or carcass
- Water

Instructions

1. Prepare your pressure canner according to your manufacturer's instructions.
2. Prepare your chicken stock by removing all meat from the bones or carcass. (The bones can also be roasted for one hour to get a darker and better tasting chicken stock).

135

3. Place the bones or carcass in a pot and fill up with water, then boil and cover, and allow to simmer for 45 minutes. Alternatively, you can use a pressure cooker, add sufficient water to cover the bones. Cook for half and hour on a pressure between 13-15 pounds.

4. Strain the bones in a big bowl, and remove any loosened meat from the bones.

5. Refrigerate the chicken stock overnight.

6. Next morning, remove any fat accumulated overnight at the top.

7. Reboil the chicken stock and pour into the jars maintaining a headspace of one inch.

8. Wipe the rim of the jars and tighten.

9. Load the jars inside the pressure canner.

15. If you use a weighted gauge canner, process the jars at a pressure of 10 pounds for 20 minutes (pint), for altitudes above 1,000 ft. If you use a dial gauge canner, process the jars for 25 minutes (quart.) at a pressure of 11 pounds. Adjust altitudes if necessary

16. When the processing time is complete, turn off the heat and allow the pressure canner to depressurize completely.

17. Unload your jars from the pressure canner and check the seals thoroughly. If any jar is not properly sealed, refrigerate and consume immediately.

Vegetable Stock

Ingredients

- One onion
- One tablespoon of olive oil
- One teaspoon of salt
- One bunch if green onion (chopped)
- Two large carrots
- Two quarts of water
- Two stalks of celery
- Two bay leaves
- Six sprigs of fresh thyme
- Eight sprigs of fresh parsley
- Eight cloves of garlic (minced)
- Two large carrots
- Scallions
- Olive oil

Instructions

1. Prepare your pressure canner based on the manufacturer's manual.
2. Prepare the vegetables by cutting them into sizable chunks.
3. Using a big soup pot (stainless steel preferably), heat your olive oil, and add the celery, carrots, bay leaves, parsley, scallions, garlic, thyme, and onion.
4. Cook the mixture over high heat between 5-10 minutes, and stir often.

5. Add the water and salt (optional) and boil it. Reduce the heat and allow to simmer for half an hour.
6. Strain the stock, discarding the vegetables.
7. Fill up the jars with the strained stock using a canning funnel, while maintaining a headspace of one inch.
8. Wipe the rims clean and tighten the jars.
9. Load your jars inside the pressure canner, turn on heat and allow to boil.
10. Allow the steam to vent for 10 minutes, then close the vent by placing your canning weight guage/ regulator (for the dial guage pressure canner).
11. For a weighted gauge canner, process the jars at a pressure of 10 pounds for 25 minutes (quarts), and 20 minutes for pints. For a dial gauge canner, process at a pressure of 11 pounds for 25 minutes (quarts) , and 20 minutes for pints. Adjust for altitudes.
12. When the processing time is complete, turn off the heat and allow the pressure canner to depressurize completely.
13. Unload the jars with a jar lifter from the pressure canner.

14. Thoroughly check the seals, and if any seal is damaged, refrigerate and use immediately.
15. Properly canned and sealed jars can be stored for 12 months on the shelf.

Chili Con Carne

Ingredients

- One teaspoon of black pepper
- One cup of onion (chopped)
- Two quarts of tomatoes (crushed or whole)
- Three pounds of beef
- Three-six tablespoons of chili powder
- Three cups of red kidney beans or dried pinto
- Five cups of water
- Five teaspoons of salt
- One cup of chopped pepper (this is optional)

Recipe yield: Nine pints

Instructions

1. Prepare your pressure canner based on the manufacturer's instructiwater
2. Prepare your beans by washing them thoroughly and placing them in a saucepan.
3. Add cold water to the beans 1-3 inches higher than the beans level, then soak between 12-18 hours.
4. Drain the beans and discard the water. Then pour 5 cups of water and 2 teaspoons of salt inside the beans, then boil.
5. Reduce the heat and allow it to simmer for about 30 minutes. Then drain and discard the water.

6. Brown the chopped onions, ground beef, and pepper if you desire in a skillet, and drain off the fats.
7. Add the tomatoes, salt, pepper, drained cooked beans, and chili powder. Then allow to simmer for 5 minutes. Ensure it doesn't thicken
8. Fill up the jars while maintaining a headspace of one inch.
9. Load the jars inside the pressure canner using a jar lifter, turn on the heat and bring to a boil.
10. For a weighted gauge canner, process the jars at a pressure of 10 pounds for 75 minutes for pints. For a dial gauge canner, process at a pressure of 11 pounds for 75 minutes for pints as shown below. Adjust atlitude if necessary.
11. When the processing time is complete turn off the heat and allow the pressure canner to depressurize completely.
12. Unload the jars with a jar lifter from the pressure canner.
13. Thoroughly check the seals, and if any seal is damaged, refrigerate and use immediately.
14. Properly canned and sealed jars can be stored for 12 months on the shelf.

Table 1. Recommended process time for **Chile Con Carne** in a dial-gauge pressure canner.

Style of Pack	Jar Size	Process Time	Canner Pressure (PSI) at Altitudes of			
			0 - 2,000 ft	2,001 - 4,000 ft	4,001 - 6,000 ft	6,001 - 8,000 ft
Hot	Pints	75 min	11 lb	12 lb	13 lb	14 lb

Table 2. Recommended process time for **Chile Con Carne** in a weighted-gauge pressure canner.

Style of Pack	Jar Size	Process Time	Canner Pressure (PSI) at Altitudes of	
			0 - 1,000 ft	Above 1,000 ft
Hot	Pints	75 min	10 lb	15 lb

143

Conclusion

One major way of saving time when preparing your food is by embracing pressure canning, meaning you don't have to prepare your favorite meals afresh every time you crave them. And while the safety of the food we consume is vital, some of the canned foods we consume are unhealthy due to the preservatives and the process of canning them. However, when you pressure can your food at home, you are sure of what you are eating. Food contamination can be life-threatening, and having the right information with step-by-step instructions on how to prepare and can your meat, broths, soups, stocks, and vegetables is key to healthy living.

All you need to know about pressure canning has been explained in simple terms in this book; so I hope you find this simple guide both fun and fulfilling.

I wish you all the best!